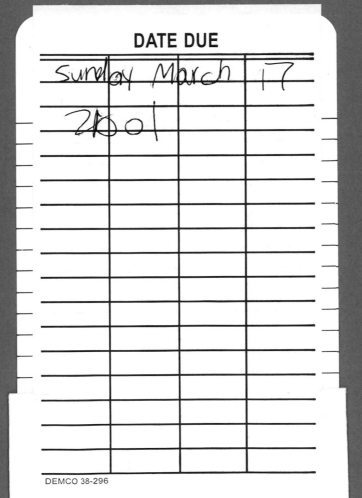

DATE DUE

Sunday March		17
2001		

DEMCO 38-296

Learning Is Fun!

KATHY ROSS C•R•A•F•T•S
NUMBERS

by Kathy Ross

Illustrated by Jan Barger

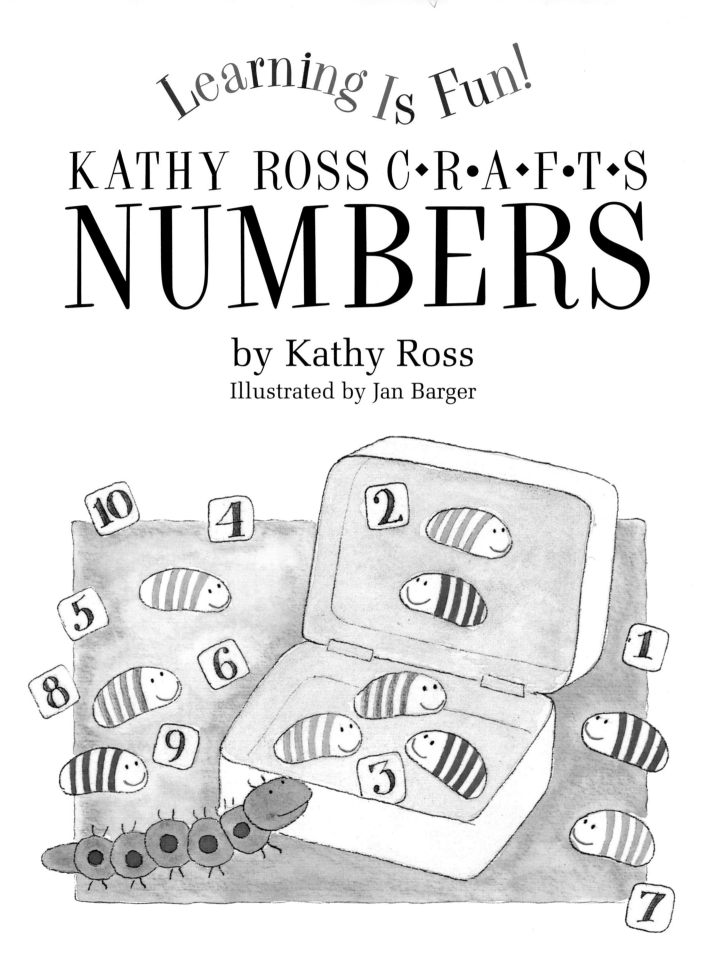

The Millbrook Press
Brookfield, Connecticut

To my number 1 grandchild—she's a 10!
K.R.

Library of Congress Cataloging-in-Publication Data
Ross, Kathy (Katharine Reynolds), 1948-
Kathy Ross crafts numbers / Kathy Ross ; illustrated by Jan Barger.
p. cm. — (Learning is fun)
Contents: One and only me—Bathtub boat and two of each crayon animals—Three
number 3 bear —Four-leaf clover lucky necklace—Five-point star magnet—Six 6's bug—
Seven-day story—Eight number 8 bunnies—Count to nine caterpillar—Ten in an
envelope bed—Gift bag house—Play cell phone—Play alarm clock—Coin family
puppets—Stamp saver—Mama foot-long worm and her twelve baby inchworms—
Calendar markers—Age cake—Caterpillar counters.
ISBN 0-7613-2105-5 (lib. bdg.) — ISBN 0-7613-1697-3 (pbk.)
1. Handicraft—Juvenile literature. 2. Numbers in art—Juvenile literature.
[1. Handicraft. 2. Numbers in art] I. Barger, Jan, 1948– ill. II. Title. III. Learning is fun!
(Brookfield, Conn.)
TT160. R7142343 2003   745.5—dc21   2002002399

Published by
The Millbrook Press, Inc.
2 Old New Milford Road
Brookfield, Connecticut 06804
www.millbrookpress.com

Printed in the United States of America
lib: 5 4 3 2 1
pbk: 5 4 3 2 1

Table of Contents

KATHY ROSS C·R·A·F·T·S
NUMBERS

Turn number one into the one and only you!

one and only dog ↓

1 and only me!

one and only cat ↓

One and Only Me

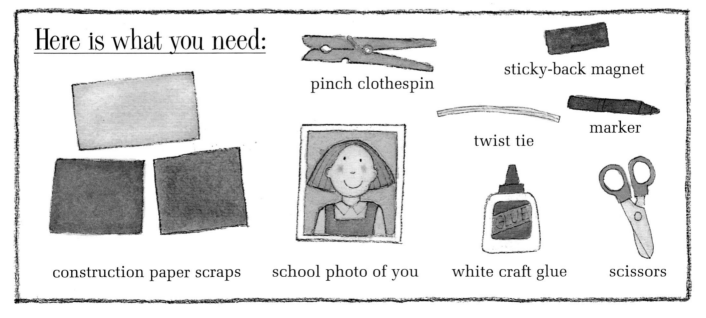

Here is what you need:

pinch clothespin

sticky-back magnet

twist tie

marker

construction paper scraps

school photo of you

white craft glue

scissors

Here is what you do:

1. Cut a number 1 from construction paper just big enough to cover one side of the clothespin.

2. Glue the twist tie across the clothespin so that the ends stick out on each side to form arms. Glue the number 1 on the twist tie for the body.

3. The pinch end of the clothespin will be the top. Cut the head from the school photo and glue it to the top of the number 1.

4. Cut feet from construction paper and glue them on the bottom of the number 1.

5. Cut a little sign from construction paper. Use the marker to write "One and Only Me" on the sign.

6. Wrap the ends of the twist tie around the ends of the sign to make it look like it is being held. Secure the ends with a dab of glue.

7. Cut a piece of sticky-back magnet to press on the back of the project so you can hang it on your refrigerator.

Use the number 1 clothespin to hold your favorite picture or school paper for display. How "one"derful!

In the story of Noah's Ark, Noah put two of each kind of animal in the ark.

Bathtub Boat and Two of Each Crayon Animals

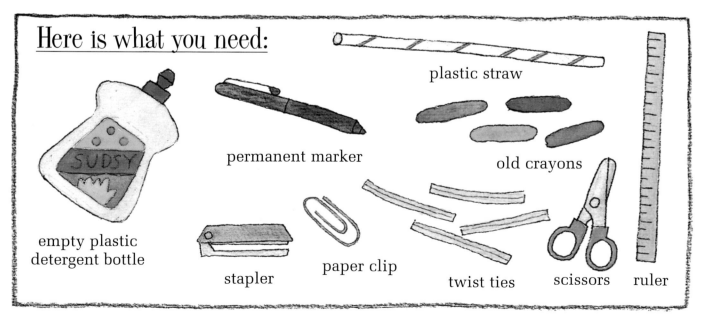

Here is what you need:

plastic straw

permanent marker

old crayons

empty plastic detergent bottle

stapler

paper clip

twist ties

scissors

ruler

Here is what you do:

1. Cut off the end of the plastic bottle about 2 inches (5 cm) from the bottom. The bottom cut from the bottle will be the boat.

2. Cut a 6-inch (15-cm) piece of plastic straw for the mast.

3. Cut a 2- by 3-inch (5- by 8-cm) piece of plastic from the remaining portion of the bottle to use for a sail.

4. Fold the sail in half and cut two small slits on the fold. Unfold the sail and slide the straw mast through the slits. Staple the mast to the boat.

5. For each pair of animals you want to make, you will need two peeled crayon pieces of the same color. It is best to use crayons that float for this project so the animals will be good swimmers if the boat tips over. Test the crayons by dropping them in water. You will find that some crayons are much better floaters than others.

6. Wrap a twist tie around the front end and the back end of the crayon to make legs for the animal. Trim off any excess twist tie, then tip the ends forward to form feet.

7. Bend out the end of the paper clip and use it to make a face in the front end of each crayon animal.

8. Use the permanent marker to write the name of your boat on the side.

Load all the **two-crayon** sets of animals into the boat and take them for a sail in your bathtub.

Use three number 3's to form the ears of the three bears.

The 3 Bears

Three Number 3 Bears

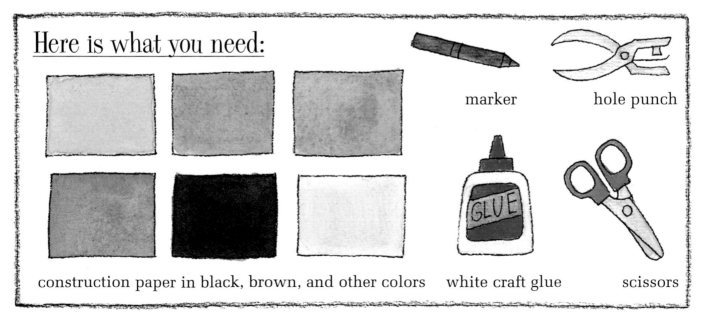

Here is what you need:

construction paper in black, brown, and other colors

marker

hole punch

white craft glue

scissors

Here is what you do:

1. Cut three number 3's from the black paper.

2. Cut three circles from the brown paper as wide as the number 3's are tall.

3. Glue the three brown circles on a sheet of construction paper for the heads of Mama, Papa, and Baby Bear.

4. Slip the ends of a number 3 under the top of each circle so that the number 3 forms ears on each bear's head.

5. Use the hole punch to punch dots from the black paper to glue on the bears to make faces.

6. Cut two triangles to make a bow tie for Papa Bear and another two in a different color to make a bow tie for Baby Bear. Cut two more triangles to glue together at the top of the head of Mama Bear for a hair bow.

You might want to use the marker to write "The 3 Bears" at the top of the picture.

If you find a clover with four leaves you are
supposed to keep it for good luck.

Four-Leaf Clover Lucky Necklace

Here is what you need:

permanent marker

lucky penny

plastic flip top from ketchup
or salad dressing bottle

green yarn or floss   white craft glue

scissors

green construction paper scrap   heart-shaped punch   yellow thin ribbon or yarn

ruler

Here is what you do:

1. Use the heart-shaped punch to punch four leaves from the green construction paper for the four-leaf clover. (If you don't have a punch, just cut four heart shapes from the paper.)

2. Glue the leaves to the center of the top of the closed cap, with the points all touching to look like a four-leaf clover.

3. Cut a tiny piece of green thread or yarn for the stem. If the yarn seems thick, unravel it and use just a strand. Glue the stem to the bottom of the four-leaf clover.

4. Open the cap. Glue the lucky penny inside the cap.

5. Use the marker to write "Good Luck" on the inside of the lid of the cap.

6. Cut a 2-foot (61-cm) length of yellow ribbon or yarn. Tie the ribbon or yarn around the hinge of the open cap, then tie the two ends together to make a necklace.

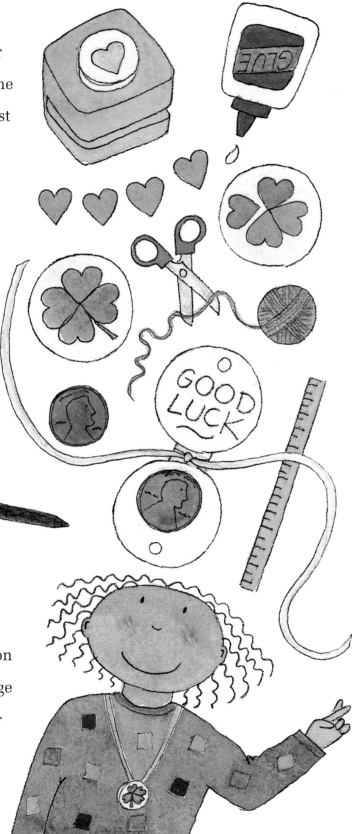

Close the lid to keep your lucky penny safe inside.

A star has five points.

Five-Point Star Magnet

Here is what you need:

wiggle eyes

tiny pom-poms

GLUE

white craft glue

sticky-back magnet

bathroom-size paper cup

scissors

yellow and red markers

red yarn

Here is what you do:

1. Cut five equally spaced slits around the paper cup from top to bottom. Each segment of the cup will become a point of the star.

2. Trim the sides of each segment of cup so that it is a triangle with the point at the top.

3. Fold each of the points of the star out from the bottom of the cup to form the star.

4. To decorate the star, color it with the marker or cover it with glue and glitter.

5. Give the star a face by gluing on the wiggle eyes and a pom-pom for a nose. Make a mouth by gluing on a piece of red yarn or draw one using the red marker.

6. Press a piece of sticky-back magnet to the back of the star.

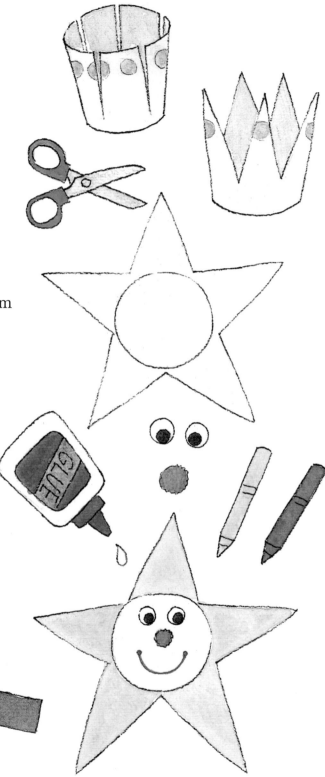

These stars are fun to decorate. I've given you some ideas, but I bet you can think of even more ways to make them pretty, so you'll probably want to make lots of them!

An insect has six legs.

Six 6's Bug

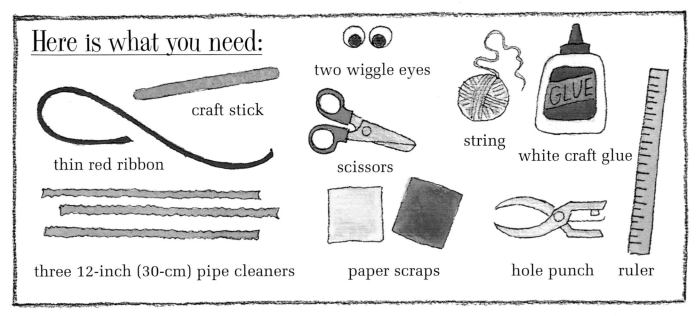

Here is what you need:

two wiggle eyes

craft stick

thin red ribbon

scissors

string

white craft glue

three 12-inch (30-cm) pipe cleaners

paper scraps

hole punch

ruler

Here is what you do:

1. Cut the three pipe cleaners in half so that you have six 6-inch (15-cm) pieces of pipe cleaner.

2. Shape each of the six pipe cleaners into the number 6.

3. Glue the round ends of three number 6 pipe cleaners together so that they overlap and the tops of the numbers stick out on one side to form the legs of the insect. Glue the second set of pipe cleaner numbers together in the same way.

4. Glue the round ends of the second set of numbers over the first set so that the three stems stick out on the opposite side to form the second set of legs for the bug.

5. Shape the legs by bending them slightly in the middle.

6. Glue two wiggle eyes on top of the bug at one end.

7. Cut a strip of red ribbon for a tongue. Cut a small triangle from one end of the ribbon to fork the end of the tongue. Glue the other end under the head of the bug so that it looks like it is sticking out.

8. Use the hole punch and the paper scraps to punch some spots to glue on the back of the bug.

9. Cut a 2-foot (61-cm) length of string. Tie one end of the string to the back of the bug. Glue the other end to the end of the craft stick.

Let the glue dry completely before taking the six 6's bug for a walk.

There are seven days in a week.

Sunday | Monday | Tuesday | Wednesday | Thursday | Friday | Saturday

TODAY IS →

Seven-Day Story

Here is what you need:

extra sheets of paper

january

old calendar page

GLUE

white craft glue

clamp clothespin

yarn

ruler

hole punch

large sheet of construction paper

stories from old magazines or printed off the Web

trims and rickrack

permanent marker

scissors

Here is what you do:

1. Turn the sheet of construction paper so that the long side is at the top and bottom. Fold the bottom of the paper up so that you make a pocket with about 3 inches (8 cm) of excess paper above the pocket.

2. Open the fold and squeeze eight equally spaced lines of glue down the inside of the fold, starting at one end of the paper and ending at the opposite end. This will create seven paper pockets, one for each day of the week.

3. Fold the paper closed again over the glue and let it dry.

4. Cut the names of the seven days of the week from the old calendar page.

5. Glue the days across the top of the paper with one over each pocket top, in the correct order, starting with Sunday.

6. Punch two holes in the top of the paper. Cut a 2-foot (61-cm) piece of yarn. Thread the yarn through the two holes and tie the ends together to make a hanger.

7. Decorate the front of the pockets with rows of trims and rickrack.

8. Use the permanent marker to write "Today is" and draw an arrow on the clothespin so that when you clip it to the bottom of the paper it will point up to the day above it.

9. Cut the story you have chosen into seven sections and number each one. Fold the sections of story and put them in the pockets in the correct order.

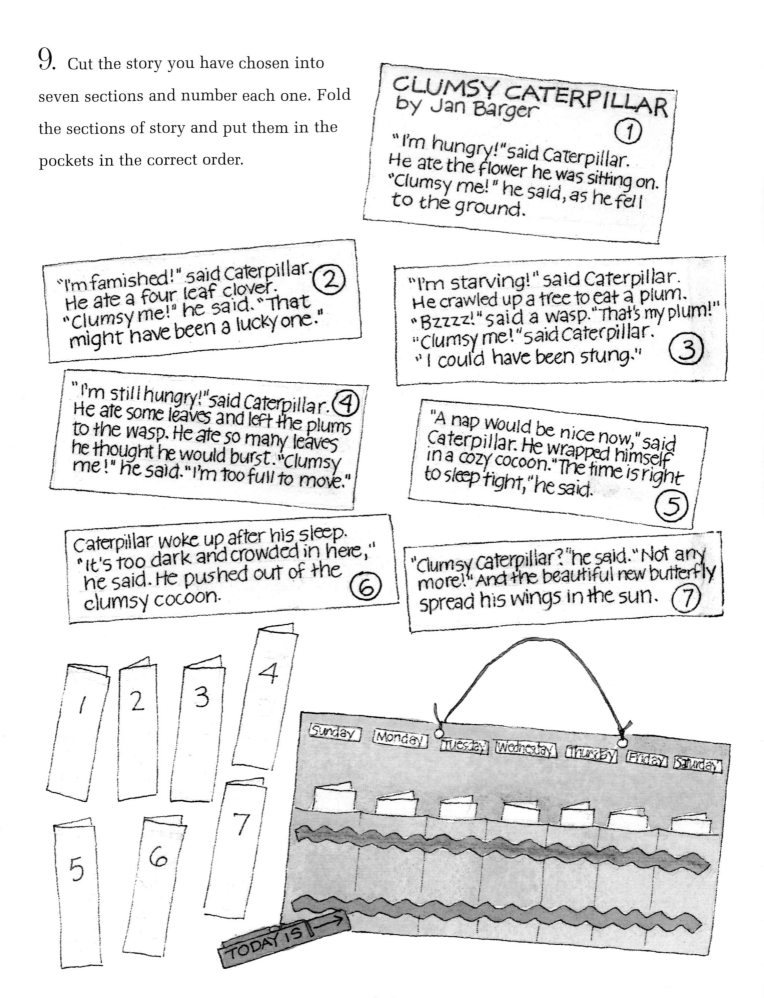

CLUMSY CATERPILLAR
by Jan Barger
(1)
"I'm hungry!" said Caterpillar. He ate the flower he was sitting on. "Clumsy me!" he said, as he fell to the ground.

"I'm famished!" said Caterpillar. (2) He ate a four leaf clover. "Clumsy me!" he said. "That might have been a lucky one."

"I'm starving!" said Caterpillar. He crawled up a tree to eat a plum. "Bzzzz!" said a wasp. "That's my plum!" "Clumsy me!" said Caterpillar. (3) "I could have been stung."

"I'm still hungry!" said Caterpillar. (4) He ate some leaves and left the plums to the wasp. He ate so many leaves he thought he would burst. "Clumsy me!" he said. "I'm too full to move."

"A nap would be nice now," said Caterpillar. He wrapped himself in a cozy cocoon. "The time is right to sleep tight," he said. (5)

Caterpillar woke up after his sleep. "It's too dark and crowded in here," he said. He pushed out of the (6) clumsy cocoon.

"Clumsy Caterpillar?" he said. "Not any more!" And the beautiful new butterfly spread his wings in the sun. (7)

Sunday Monday Tuesday Wednesday Thursday Friday Saturday

TODAY IS

10. Starting on Sunday, put the clothespin on the correct day and take out the first part of the story to read. You might want to glue each section of the story to a sheet of paper and draw some illustrations of your own around it. At the end of the week you can tie the pages together for a book.

This **seven-day calendar** is a nice gift to make for a younger child. A new story can be put in each week. If you are going to use it yourself, it might be fun to do it with a friend and each choose a surprise story to put in for the other.

Make a charming greeting card decorated
with eight number 8 bunnies.

Eight Number 8 Bunnies

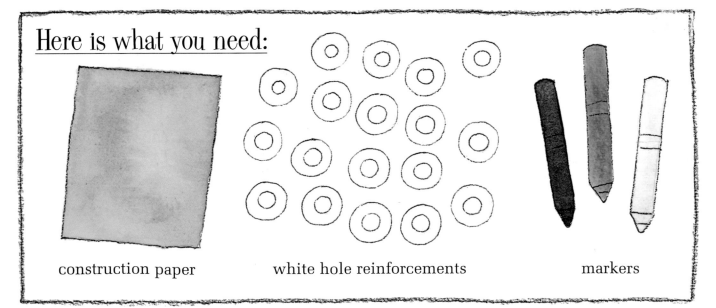

Here is what you need:

construction paper   white hole reinforcements   markers

Here is what you do:

1. Fold a sheet of construction paper in half to make a card.

2. To make each bunny, stick two hole reinforcements on the card with the edges touching.

3. Use a marker to add eyes, ears, nose, whiskers, and a tail to each bunny.

4. You might also want to use markers to add such details as grass and carrots to the area surrounding the bunnies.

5. Use two hole reinforcements to make a number 8 at the top of the card, then write the word "bunnies" after it.

6. Use markers to write your greeting or message inside the card and sign your name.

This project makes a clever "get well" card or thank you note.

This caterpillar has nine segments.

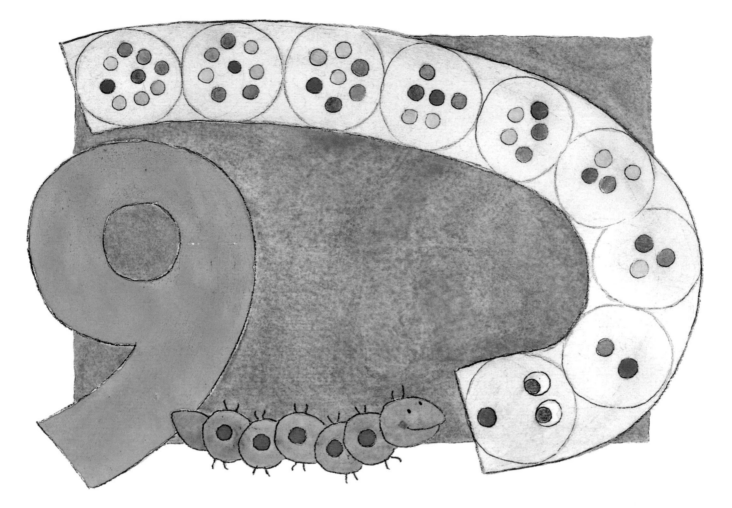

Count to Nine Caterpillar

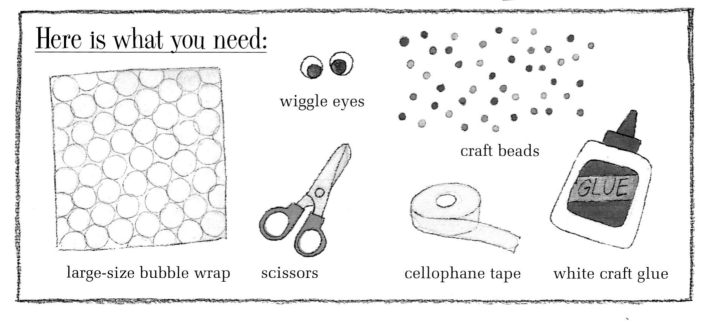

Here is what you need:

large-size bubble wrap   wiggle eyes   craft beads   scissors   cellophane tape   white craft glue

Here is what you do:

1. Cut a strip of bubble wrap with nine bubbles in a row for the caterpillar. You can tape two strips together if you need to.

2. Cut a tiny slit in the flat bottom of each bubble.

3. Put one bead in the first bubble, two in the second, and so on until you get to the last bubble, which will have nine beads in it.

4. Gently pull the ends of the bubble strip to puff the bubbles up again with air.

5. Cover the slit in the bottom of each bubble with cellophane tape.

6. Glue two wiggle eyes to the end of the bubble with one bead in it.

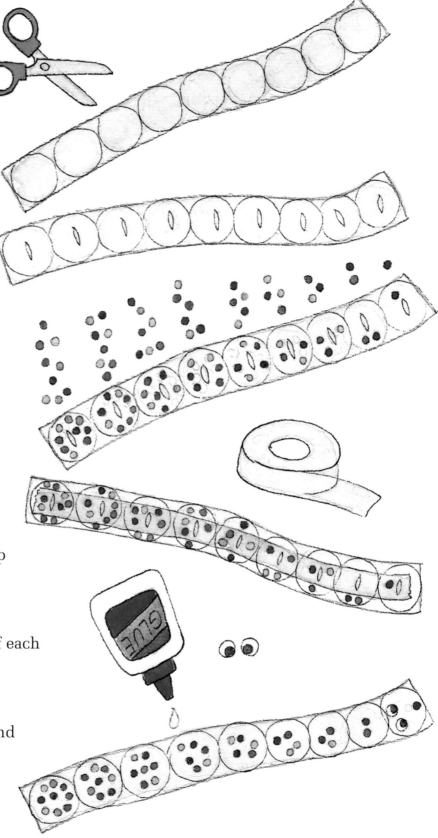

This **nine-segment caterpillar** is happy crawling across a desk or taped to the wall.

Make this project to use when you sing
the silly song "Ten in Bed."

Ten in an Envelope Bed

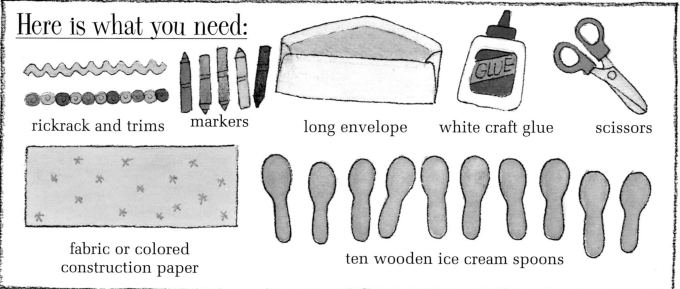

Here is what you need:

rickrack and trims   markers   long envelope   white craft glue   scissors

fabric or colored
construction paper

ten wooden ice cream spoons

Here is what you do:

1. Open the flap of the envelope to become the head-board of the bed. Glue rickrack or trim to the edge of the head-board to decorate it.

2. Cut a piece of fabric or colored paper to glue over the envelope below the flap to look like a blanket. Glue trim across the top of the blanket.

3. Decorate the ten sticks to look like ten different characters, people, or animals. Draw faces on the spoon end of each stick and color each handle for the body with the markers.

4. Put the ten characters in a row inside the envelope bed.

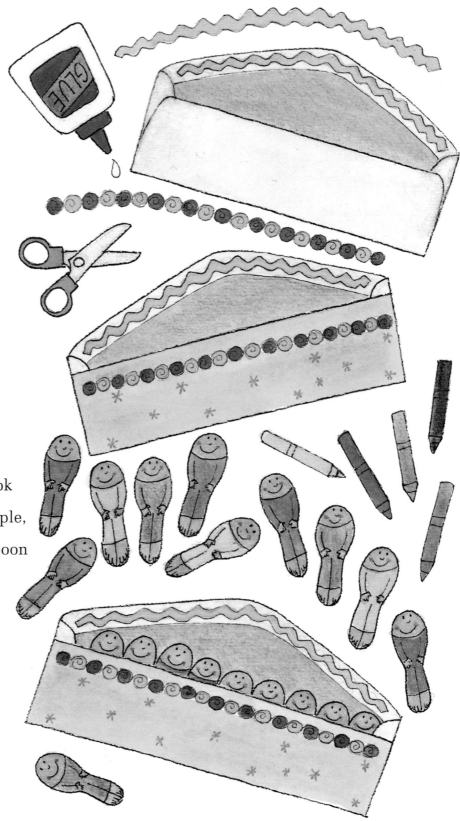

As you sing the song "Ten in Bed," remove one character each time you sing "they all rolled over and one fell out."

The house or building where you live
has numbers on it to help people find it.

Gift Bag House

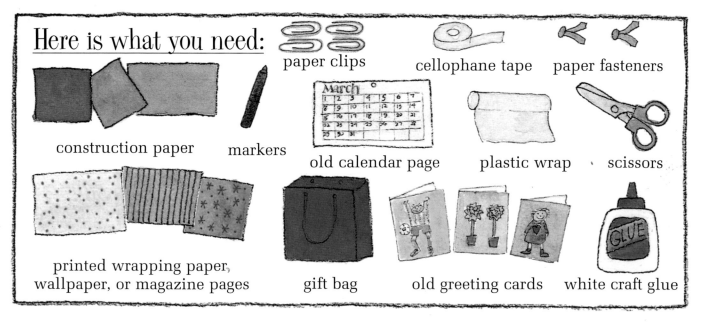

Here is what you need:

paper clips

cellophane tape

paper fasteners

construction paper

markers

old calendar page

plastic wrap

scissors

printed wrapping paper,
wallpaper, or magazine pages

gift bag

old greeting cards

white craft glue

Here is what you do:

1. Cut windows and a double door from one side of the bag. The double door will make it easier to work inside the bag house.

2. Tape plastic wrap behind the windows to look like glass.

3. Attach a paper fastener to each door for the doorknobs.

4. Line the inside walls of the bag house by gluing on printed paper. You can use a pattern to look like wallpaper or cut an actual room scene out of a magazine.

5. Cover the floor of the house by gluing a piece of construction paper over the bottom of the bag.

6. Tape the top of the bag house closed. Glue a folded piece of construction paper to the top of the bag for a roof.

7. Cut a chimney for the roof from construction paper. Add detail to the chimney with a marker, then glue the chimney to the top of one side of the roof.

8. Cut the numbers of your own house from the calendar page. Glue the numbers to a small piece of construction paper. Glue the paper to the house above the door.

9. Cut details to glue to the front of the house from old greeting cards or magazine pages. You could add shrubs or flowers and birds or other animals.

10. To make people to live in the house cut figures from greeting cards. To make a stand for each figure, bend the outside loop of a paper clip down at a right angle. Tape the smaller loop to the back of the figure.

You might want to **add more things** to the bag house such as curtains and furniture.

If you want to phone someone you will need
to know the correct phone number.

Play Cell Phone

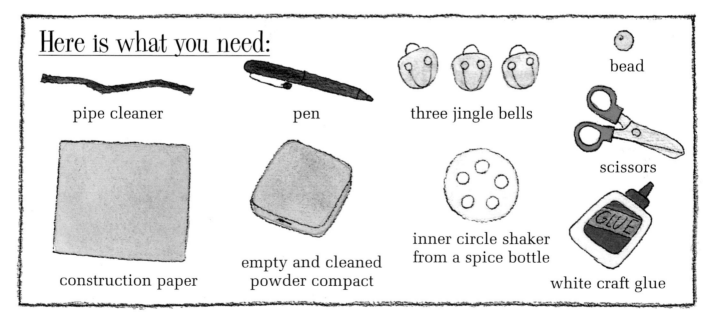

Here is what you need:

pipe cleaner

pen

three jingle bells

bead

construction paper

empty and cleaned
powder compact

inner circle shaker
from a spice bottle

scissors

white craft glue

Here is what you do:

1. Press a piece of construction paper into the powder section of the compact to shape the paper. Cut the shape out.

2. Use the pen to draw the squares with the numbers and signs on them just like a real telephone.

3. Glue the numbered paper in the powder section of the compact.

4. Glue the circle from the spice bottle over the mirror section of the compact for the earphone.

5. Thread the jingle bells on the pipe cleaner. Wrap the pipe cleaner around the hinged section of the compact. Twist one end of the pipe cleaner around itself on one side of the outside of the hinge to secure it, with the jingle bells on the outside of the compact.

6. Slide a bead over the other end of the pipe cleaner and fold the end down to secure the bead. This will be the antenna for the cell phone. Fold it down next to the compact unless you need it to make a call.

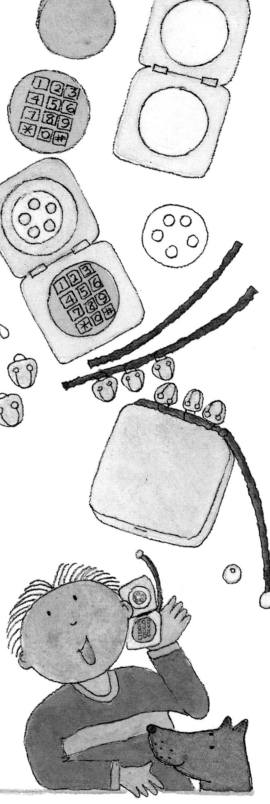

To make your cell phone "ring" just give it a shake. Pull up the antenna and open it up to take a phone call or to make one.

We use numbers to tell time.

Play Alarm Clock

Here is what you need:

red pipe cleaner

pink pom-pom

scissors

two identical plastic jar lids

three or more jingle bells

two large wiggle eyes

two large craft beads

masking tape

old calendar page

discarded compact disc (CD)

two twist ties

white craft glue

cellophane tape

Here is what you do:

1. Cut the numbers 1 through 12 from the calendar page. Glue the numbers around the edge of the CD to look like a clock.

2. Trim one end of each of the twist ties to a point for the two clock hands. Arrange the two hands on the front of the clock for the time you get up in the morning. Bend the ends of the hands back through the hole in the center of the CD and secure them with glue and masking tape.

3. Give the clock a face by gluing on the two wiggle eyes, the pom-pom for a nose, and a piece of the red pipe cleaner for a smile.

4. Thread the jingle bells on a piece of pipe cleaner. Tape the two ends of the pipe cleaner inside one of the plastic lids so that the bells are not touching the lid and can ring freely.

5. Use the cellophane tape to tape the two plastic lids together with the insides facing each other to create a case for the jingle bells.

6. Glue the clock face to one side of the bell case with the bottom edge of the clock even with the edge of the case.

7. Glue a bead to the case on each side of the clock face to help it stand.

Give the play clock a shake to make the alarm "ring."

33

Different coins represent different numbers of pennies.

Coin Family Puppets

Here is what you need:

tiny stickers, jewels, sequins, and buttons

¢50 PENNIES 50¢

coin wrapper for pennies

$2 NICKELS 2$

coin wrapper for nickels

$5 DIMES 5$

coin wrapper for dimes

white craft glue

scissors

yarn

cellophane tape

$10 QUARTERS 10$

coin wrapper for quarters

a penny, nickel, dime, and quarter

Here is what you do:

1. The face on each coin will become the face of each finger puppet. Tape a coin to the top of the correct wrapper with the face side out.

2. Glue yarn bits to the top of each coin for hair.

3. Glue one small item to the penny wrapper finger puppet below the face to represent one penny. Glue five small things to the nickel finger puppet to represent five pennies. Glue ten small things to the dime finger puppet to represent ten pennies. Glue twenty-five small things to the quarter puppet to represent twenty-five pennies.

You may want to make a half-dollar finger puppet, too, but you will have to glue fifty tiny things on that one!

The number on a postage stamp tells how many pennies it cost.

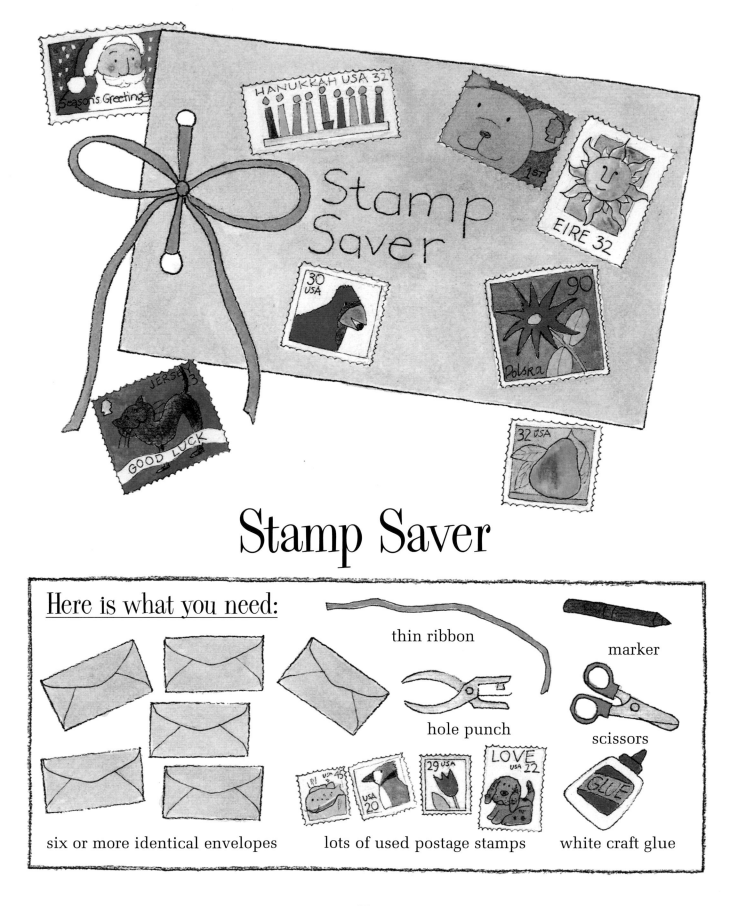

Stamp Saver

Here is what you need:

thin ribbon

marker

hole punch

scissors

six or more identical envelopes

lots of used postage stamps

white craft glue

Here is what you do:

1. Cut the flaps off the envelopes and stack them with the address side up on all except the last one. Punch two holes on the left side of the envelopes so that you can tie them into a book.

2. Tie the envelopes loosely together with a piece of the thin ribbon.

3. Write "stamp saver" on the front envelope with the marker. Decorate the envelope with some of your favorite stamps.

4. See which stamp numbers you have a lot of. Glue a different number stamp to the front of each envelope page and store the rest inside.

5. Store extra odd stamps inside the front and back covers. It is easy to add more pages to the stamp saver book as you collect additional stamps.

Saving **stamps** is fun, and they can be used for all sorts of craft projects.

We use numbers to tell the size of things.

Mama Foot-Long Worm and Her Twelve Baby Inchworms

Here is what you need:

two large wiggle eyes

twenty-four small wiggle eyes

rickrack in two colors   white craft glue   scissors   ruler

Here is what you do:

1. Cut a foot-long (30-cm) piece of rickrack for the mother worm. Glue the two large wiggle eyes back-to-back over one end of the rickrack.

2. Cut twelve 1-inch (2.5-cm) pieces of rickrack for the twelve baby worms.

3. Glue two small wiggle eyes, back-to-back, over one end of each piece to make a baby worm.

4. Line the babies up end to end. The twelve babies together will be the same length as the foot-long mother worm.

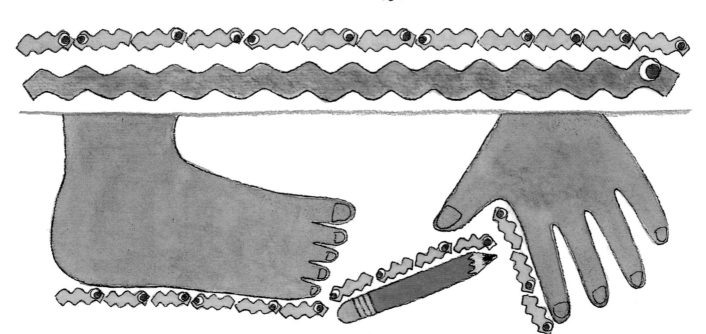

How many **baby inchworms** long is your foot? Your pencil? Your finger? If something is longer than 12 inches (30 cm), you can use the mother worm and some of her babies to help measure it.

The numbers on a calendar help us count the days in each month.

Calendar Markers

Here is what you need:

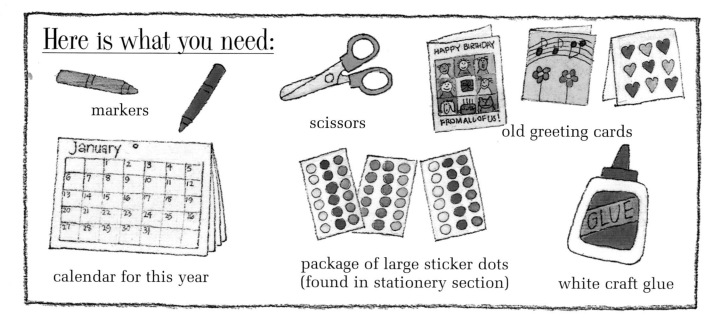

markers

scissors

old greeting cards

calendar for this year

package of large sticker dots
(found in stationery section)

white craft glue

Here is what you do:

1. Think of all the appointments, events, and special days in the month that you would like to remember. Go through the old greeting cards to find tiny pictures to represent each event. You might want to choose a tiny heart for the birthday of someone special, an animal in a nightshirt for an overnight guest, and so on.

2. Cut each tiny picture out and glue it to a sticky dot. If there is room, you can use the markers to write something on the dot, too.

3. Stick each dot to the correct day on the calendar. You can write on the calendar under the dot, too, if you wish.

A collection of dots for holidays and birthdays makes a very nice gift for someone.

We tell our age by counting how many years old we are.

Age Cake

Here is what you need:

pipe cleaner

pin back

felt scrap

rickrack

cake candies

corrugated cardboard

colored craft glues   white craft glue   scissors   ruler

Here is what you do:

1. Cut a 3-inch– (8-cm–) wide cake shape from the corrugated cardboard with the holes running up and down.

2. Cut an oval plate for the cake from the felt scrap. Glue the cake to the felt plate.

3. Use the rickrack, cake candies, and colored glue to decorate the cake.

4. Cut a 1-inch (2.5-cm) pipe cleaner candle for each year old you are. Cut some extras so you can add them in future years.

5. Put a "candle" in the corrugated cardboard at the top of the cake for each year old you are.

6. Put a dab of orange or yellow craft glue on the top of each pipe cleaner to "light" it.

7. Glue the pin back to the back of the cake.

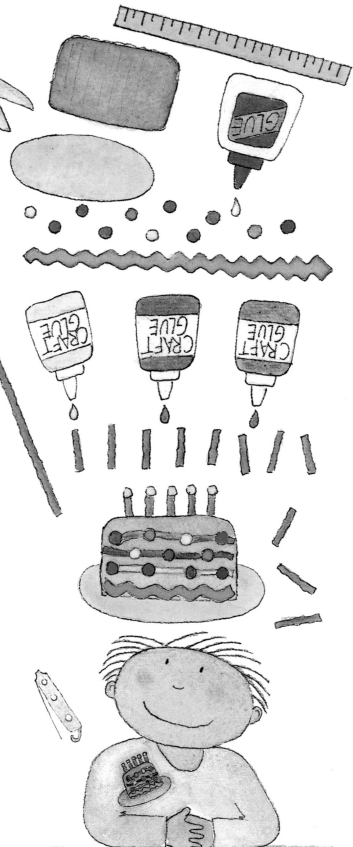

Wear the cake on your birthday—adding a new candle each year.

Make a counting box that fits in your pocket.

Caterpillar Counters

Here is what you need:

sticky-back magnet

hole punch

dry lima beans

permanent sharp-point markers

GLUE

white craft glue

small metal box such as mints come in

construction paper

old calendar page

scissors

Here is what you do:

1. Trace around the top of the tin box on the construction paper. Cut the shape out and use the markers to decorate it. Glue the paper to the top of the tin box.

2. Choose ten lima beans to make the ten caterpillars. Add a face and stripes to one side of each lima bean using the markers.

3. Punch a dot from the sticky-back magnet for each caterpillar. Stick a dot on the back of each caterpillar so that it will stick to the inside of the metal box.

4. Cut the numbers 1 to 10 from the old calendar page. Stick a piece of sticky-back magnet to the back of each number.

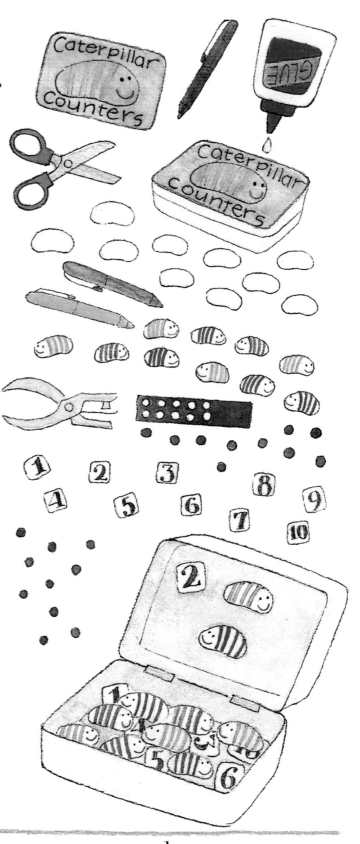

Choose a **number** to stick inside the lid. Stick the correct **number** of caterpillars next to the **number**. Store the **numbers** and the caterpillars inside the closed box.

Numbers are also found on playing cards.

Playing Card Counters

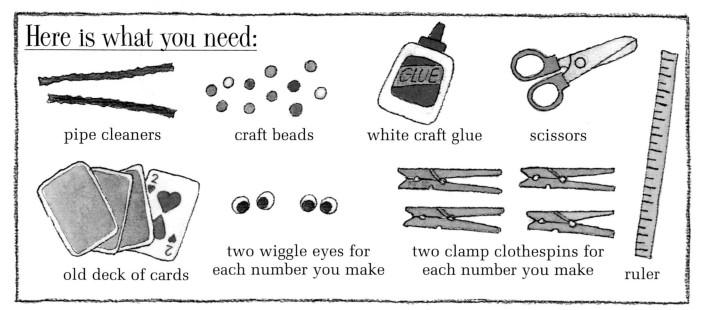

Here is what you need:

pipe cleaners   craft beads   white craft glue   scissors

old deck of cards   two wiggle eyes for each number you make   two clamp clothespins for each number you make   ruler

46

Here is what you do:

1. Choose two cards with the same number on them.

2. Cut a 6-inch (15-cm) piece of pipe cleaner for the arms. Lay the arms across the top portion of the picture side of one card. Cover the card and pipe cleaner with glue. Set the second card, picture side down, over the first card. The numbers should be on the outside of the cards and the pipe cleaner should now stick out on both sides of the card for arms.

3. Glue two wiggle eyes and a craft bead nose at the top of one side of the cards.

4. Clamp two clothespins to the bottom of the cards for the legs.

5. Slide the correct number of craft beads on the pipe cleaner arms to match the number on the cards.

Make a card counter for each number in the deck of cards.

About the Author and Artist

Twenty-five years as a teacher and director of nursery school programs has given Kathy Ross extensive experience in guiding young children through craft projects. Among the more than forty craft books she has written are CRAFTS FOR ALL SEASONS, MAKE YOURSELF A MONSTER, THE BEST BIRTHDAY PARTIES EVER, THE BEST CHRISTMAS CRAFTS EVER, and THE STORYTIME CRAFT BOOK. She is also the author of the popular *Holiday Crafts for Kids* series, and the *Crafts for Kids Who Are Wild About . . .* series.

Learn more about Kathy and download new crafts by visiting kathyross.com

Jan Barger, originally from Little Rock, Arkansas, now lives in Plumpton, East Sussex, England, with her husband and their cocker spaniel, Tosca. As well as writing and illustrating children's books, she designs greeting cards, sings with the Brighton Festival Chorus, and plays piccolo with the Sinfonia of Arun.

Kathy and Jan together have created the other books in this series: KATHY ROSS CRAFTS LETTER SHAPES; KATHY ROSS CRAFTS LETTER SOUNDS; KATHY ROSS CRAFTS TRIANGLES, RECTANGLES, CIRCLES, AND SQUARES; and KATHY ROSS CRAFTS COLORS.